ANIMALIA
Graeme Base

Within the pages of this book
You may discover, if you look
Beyond the spell of written words,
A hidden land of beasts and birds.

For many things are 'of a kind',
And those with keenest eyes will find
A thousand things, or maybe more –
It's up to you to keep the score.

A final word before we go;
There's one more thing you ought to know:
In Animalia, you see,
It's possible you might find *me*.

– Graeme

For Robyn

VIKING

Published by the Penguin Group Melbourne, London, New York, Toronto, Dublin, Auckland, Johannesburg, New Delhi, Beijing.
First published, under Viking Kestrel imprint, by Penguin Books Australia Ltd 1986.
25 27 29 30 28 26 24
Copyright © Doublebase Pty Ltd, 1986

Transparencies by Latrobe Colourlab, Melbourne
Colour separations by CS Graphic Reproduction Pty Ltd,
Melbourne
Printed in China

ISBN: 978 0 670 81536 4
penguin.com.au

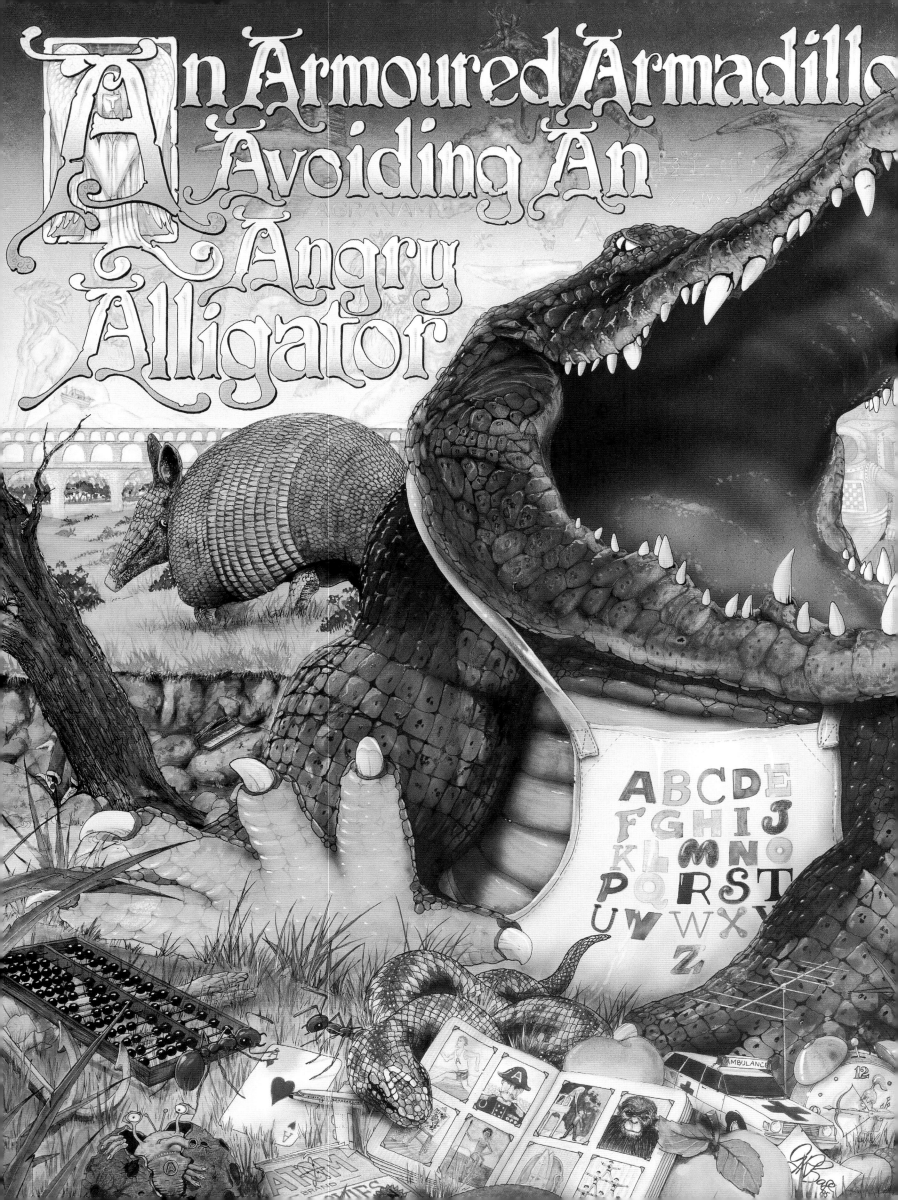

An Armoured Armadillo Avoiding An Angry Alligator

GREAT GREEN GORILLAS
GROWING GRAPES IN A
GORGEOUS GLASS GREENHOUSE

Horrible hairy hogs hurrying homeward on heavily-harnessed horses

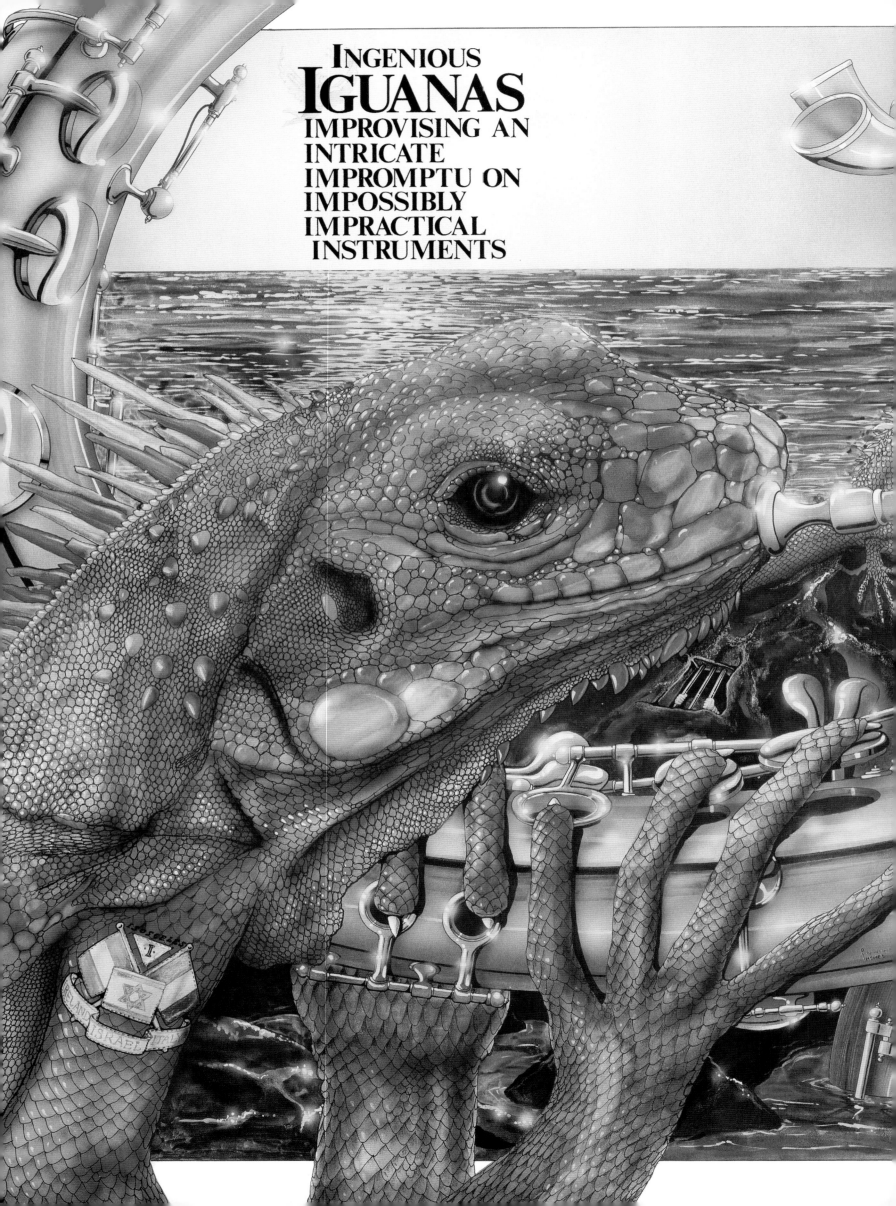

INGENIOUS
IGUANAS
IMPROVISING AN INTRICATE IMPROMPTU ON IMPOSSIBLY IMPRACTICAL INSTRUMENTS

JOVIAL · JACKALS · JUGGLING · JUGS · OF · JELLY · IN · THE · JUNGLE

Nine Nautical Newts
Navigating
Near Norway

ONE
OUTRAGEOUS
OLD
OSTRICH
ORDERING
AN
ONION
OMELETTE

Proud Peacocks
Preening
Perfect
Plumage

Quivering Quails Queuing Quietly for Quills

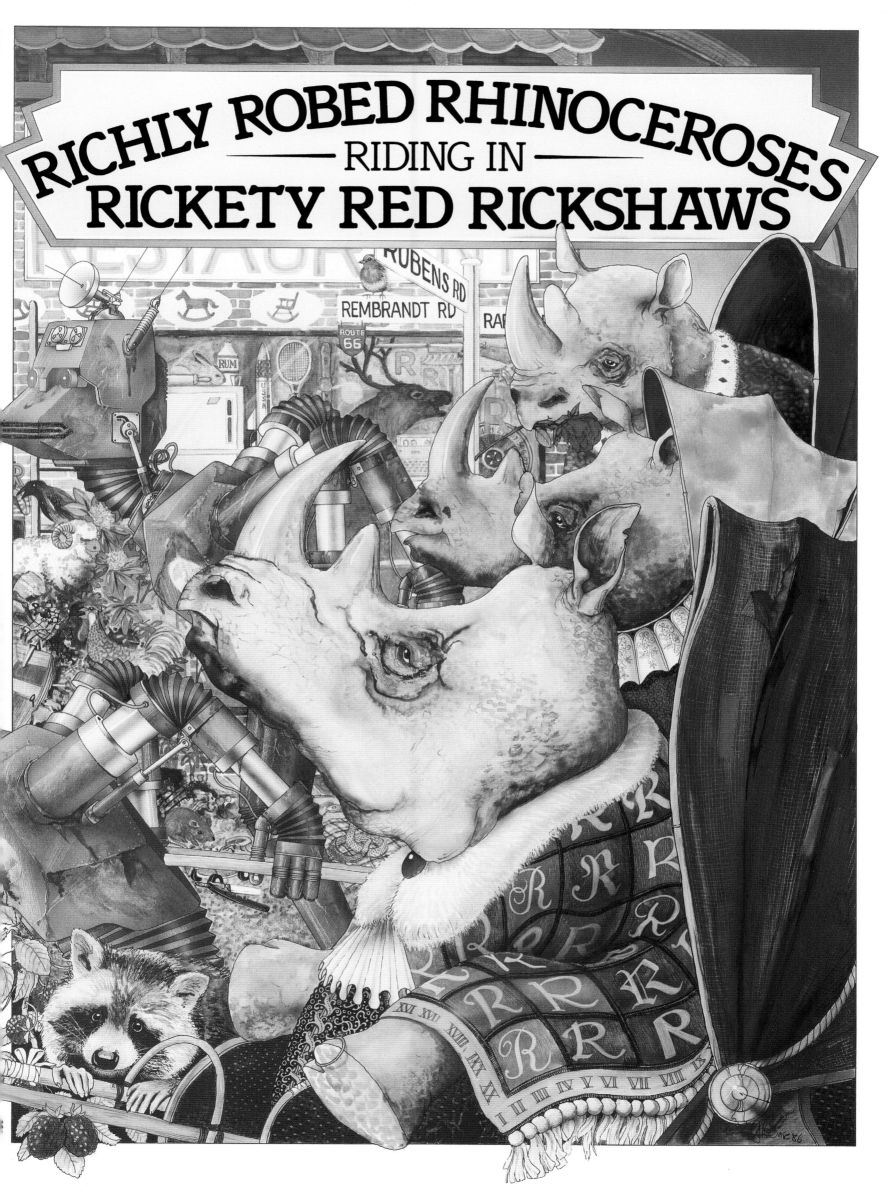

SIX · SLITHERING · SNAKES

TWO TIGERS TAKING THE 10.20 TRAIN TO TIMBUKTU

UNRULY UNICORNS UPENDING URNS OF ULTRAMARINE UMBRELLAS

Wicked Warrior WASPS wildly waving Warlike Weapons

YOUTHFUL YAKS YODELLING
IN YELLOW YACHTS

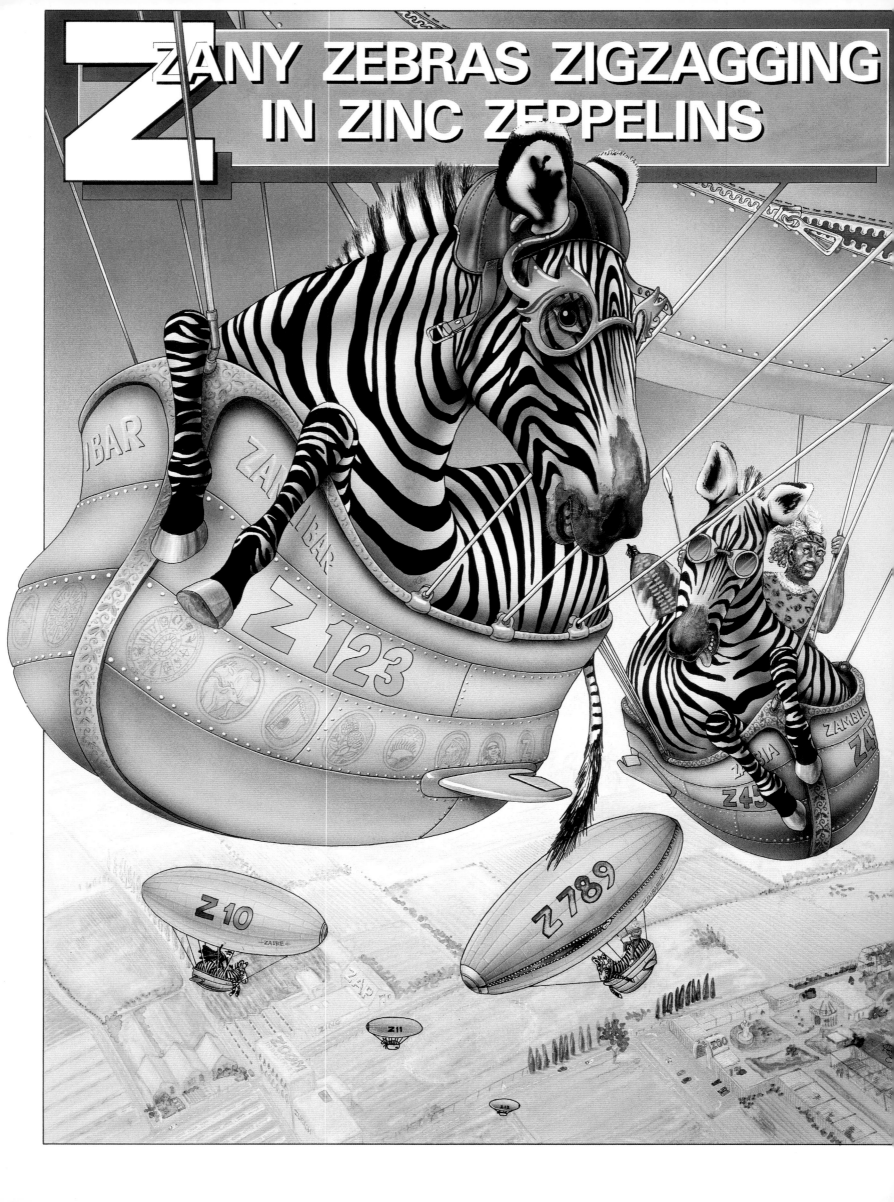

ZANY ZEBRAS ZIGZAGGING IN ZINC ZEPPELINS